SLINKY NAIVE

Slinky Naive

CAROLINE SZPAK

poems

[ANVIL PRESS • 2018]

Copyright © 2018 by Caroline Szpak

Anvil Press Publishers Inc.
P.O. Box 3008, Main Post Office
Vancouver, B.C. V6B 3X5 CANADA
www.anvilpress.com

All rights reserved. No part of this book may be reproduced by any means without the prior written permission of the publisher, with the exception of brief passages in reviews. Any request for photocopying or other reprographic copying of any part of this book must be directed in writing to Access Copyright: The Canadian Copyright Licensing Agency, One Yonge Street, Suite 800, Toronto, Ontario, Canada, M5E 1E5.

Library and Archives Canada Cataloguing in Publication

    Szpak, Caroline, author
        Slinky naive / Caroline Szpak. — First edition.

    Poems.
    ISBN 978-1-77214-115-3 (softcover)

        I. Title.

PS8637.Z63S65 2018   C811'.6   C2018-901888-7

Printed and bound in Canada
Cover design by Rayola Graphic Design
Interior by HeimatHouse
Represented in Canada by Publishers Group Canada
Distributed by Raincoast Books

The publisher gratefully acknowledges the financial assistance of the Canada Council for the Arts, the Government of Canada, and the Province of British Columbia through the B.C. Arts Council and the Book Publishing Tax Credit.

"On certain days the meteorological metaphor moves toward an actual representation. At such times the swollen matter of the clouds resembles the folds of the human brain."

— Andrzej Stasiuk, *Dukla*, "Sky"

"—What is that, Mr. Dedalus? the quaker librarian asked. Was it a celestial phenomenon?
—A star by night, Stephen said. A pillar of the cloud by day."

— James Joyce, *Ulysses*

CONTENTS

Grandfathers of Bogatynia 9
The Pomeranian Front 10
Krapkowice 12
Bleached Wieliczka 13
Black Madonna 15
Zgorzelec 16
Examen 17
A Trophy Atrophy 20
Biochemical Romance 23
Pseudo-Plastic Fluid 25
Requisition Villain 28
Somatosensory Evoked 29
Aftercare 30
As Aspirated 32
Bone Density 33
French Revolution 34
Music for Two or More Turtles 35
Form Intake 37
Lysis and Registration 38
Save the Date 42
Alternate Rebellion 43
Hydraulic Gretel Nocturne 44
Haltingly 45
Conveyor 46
Apsis 47
Planet of Things 48
What Happened in Venice 49
The Redshift 50
Afoot 52
Lovebirds I and II 53
Lithopedion Love Song 54
Everyone Loves a Slinky 56
Signs Over Symptoms 59

Organ Donor   60
Astrobleme Anodyne   62
Tenderizer   63
Under the Table   65
Old Times   67
Allostatic Load   68
Their Nurse Nautical   70
Available Emoticons   71
Dressed Fabulously in Weeds   72
The Size of Watch Movements   73
He Didn't Know Where Anything Was   74
Outliving Lanterns   75
Wouldn't Dream of It   76
The Origin of Practicality   77
Bloodshots   83
Roman Holiday   84
Do You Want My Postal Code?   85
Kept Time   86
This Possession   87
The Emperor   88
Faraday Dark Space   89
Apollinarian After   90
Passive Transgressive   92
Atomzahl   94
Atheist Staplers   95
Clouds like Ice   96
As Cold as You Thought It Was   97
Partial Nudity   98
Skin Foundation Chairs   99
Rustle Hematology   101
Mean Corpuscular Volume   102
Humour Maintenance   103
Fluency of Overbites   105

Acknowledgments   107

GRANDFATHERS OF BOGATYNIA

Everything sounds
the same from inside a plane.
Even the warm air

opens booklets, reads water
colours carbon monoxide detects.
Poor circulation meets morning

like an equal on the flood, or breath
never reaching the floor. What about
the mutual exclusion of cavities?

What about two empty chairs
facing one another? A bandage
can't outgrow the still life a subtraction

smaller than smoke from thermal
stations, but not
a water for bridges —

something he sinks
into — fewer handprints,
the difference in volts. Light sleepers

always as long as approach, initials
instead. Just write
me one gentle poem, he said.

Can you do that?

THE POMERANIAN FRONT

Where is everyone
kept out of towels
they can't find a shell
that won't crack
at Kołobrzeg
small dogs fall
upon large ones
tenderized the dugout
everything but the stake
its lines are Baltic and rough
like stepping through
my hair longer
to dry than a whimper
is chambered this crewcut
identifies the handspan
catches moths the same way
they catch the orange
light in the steam asks
for a ball gown on one less
survival skill it'd be better
for everyone with a hyphen
there's no proof like it —
the ends of your hair
pulled from the rest
of your hair
blindfolding the tissue
in your pocket a ritual
gear grazing from the text
the self-taught length
of a necktie. I'm worse
with rings the high
limit room is brighter

past your sandpaper
stands to say this enough
I'm no better
than Catherine
the Great either
hamper or let me
teal on my back oh
every waterway large
enough to eat
with its hands no red hair
to cut like the imperial
stride called the shore
small age smallpox
not the only toy soldier
I've known to crouch
these teeth to royal flush
we want to stop modern
blood flow during surgery
an expansive and final use
of grey we want it for our laps
kept away from our children
Voltaire like any freeze
good Slav the candlelight takes
itself out start with the end
of a cable *You belong*
to the State.
You belong to me.

KRAPKOWICE

This old chandelier weather
receptors like a camel I share
card sections on nights
against the pillow
a sandbox of understudies,
dressed to match
both imminent black
Alone sequel its prime
wet loom we slid
their fingers torched
of suspicion.

laden, coast lambent to indistinct
a toe, cheapen public
your eyelashes blink
displacing the pleas of silviculture
waiters in bombs
the goats they're posed beside
socks cuffed in another *Home*
of brief shoulders the first
pharmacological as widows between take
on the vanity stopwatch

BLEACHED WIELICZKA

I guess that's why
they don't call it
mouth sex no dashes
tap above the staple
factory no time
to align your slack
head with the rest
of the proscenium
sconce part of what
the salt made
it's been a river
since I've seen
all varieties of animal
print workout gear
rodents spaced
far as the flare
of nostrils lucid
as a sack your use
of foyers gets under
my cartoon suspect
number one is ingrown
there is no question
suspect number one
stacks the white
with every single shot
is there another rake
in the shed? I guess
that's why they call it
a spoke nipple in a matter
of months I became
Duchamp's Readymate
of the year

I couldn't revive
a rounded
face I thought
headlights would
dream against
the glare.

BLACK MADONNA

Częstochowa the flare
of this stray pillow
crossed off under her
arm addendum
relics dicey
tubs all the nuns
saints on both sides
of their calling
cards accordion
a crawl in residents
that feel the water
tastes sweet may be
part pigment
edible cosmetics a loss
of emphasis fine tuning
sweat must have eyelids
like a husband a school
group sells shoddy
in that mud state
launches a tour
of paradoxical
undressing the fries
flattered clay flat
it's cold on basic flush
it's time to be subsequent
half knee, rocking, or half
knee rocking, everyone
knows how to form
a crease drown it
the swimmers
are full the beds
are switched.

ZGORZELEC

They'll boast strokes
straight as posters
only outlines
aren't Neisse or is it
Nysa's wiped numbers

from their mowers
obscured they tumble
Pod Orłem like a ring
of keys stiff as necks
no nights count

wide nets of amputation
known longer than this
broken heel its lather bred
at the foot of our forgeries
never slept in klatka

on the outcry holds up
less lalka when there's another
use for the barn the state
of emergency it's easier to find
offense in dessert forks.

EXAMEN

There's burgundy and there's classic
burgundy accumulating pamphlets
like traumas, every fine distinction

tolerance ever made about big time
bruxers, their crux of light touch
evolves rapid as road salt slit

how horse hair smells, stealth
girlhood that knows when
it's too late to sneak a second winter

coat into your mouth and find
vesicles smacked against a wall
won't pass the experiment, not

the common ones, lysosomes
limber with proof
of your shorthand digest

any doctor's waiting
room when marooned
fishnets are for bent

straws, secondary
stencils can't claim
carotid dispatched

by sinews of breath
over roiling jewelry
I am told it is all

about fulcrums and I
always do what I'm told
suet and the tuning fork

at the base of your foot
the safe distance of vibration
a quiver of elbows

from sandcastles
feathered as practise
runs against the sides

of your face think
a tuning fork will
fix you or won't

turn you on to peak
plasma, virtual
vagotomies additional

creme for self-rising
gurneys sour often vagus
leaning inland by design

we can't tell if it's Pringles
or ringlets that exist
borrowed dough never

like a daughter outright
those were pastries
the molecular floor

where air conditions itself
as a mastoid tell them
to relax their legs and resist

with their knees scaling
or non-scaling storage time
how velvet

headfirst and round
a curtained
silo drops reddened.

A TROPHY ATROPHY

I've never been
to a bachelorette
there is no returning

the touch of black
organ tulips a cessation
of longhand it's just

given one discount
we call platelets
taffeta, our petite

pancetta ambient
bipedal sums lie
in various antler

insulation, bell
cursive to shoulder
hour there up

the terminus
where the gradient
hose is dimmed,

every kill screen ever
set off will flash
like a gill spreading

peripherally clearing
centrally lorded peroxide
never saved sinew

tournaments burst
at the entrance
of the ear canal

when I said cherries
undress the nails
the coastal chance

they get domestication
with underwriter enamel,
raccoons finish off

the vacuum in each
other, signet precinct
most of my sibilance

vouchers elasticity,
its cabbage slope
of evening adhesion, human

error the fatalism of a salmon
coloured cocktail dress, teeth
at their thinnest

points roll blush
through the first
stages of a wind

instrument I liked
him but never learned
to play, feared their front

hedge was a Sunday
pupil, open-holed
flute severance

if you think you're retaining
water, it's probable
if you think a nightjar is

what you felted, security
of a gland dealt its flesh
tones. I feel holographic,

a fluted litter, lecture on
the ultimate wool of sugar
mist, freeze well I hear you

crystallize one too many
times a night, gaits lance
vocabulary from every shred

of savoy they cut
her food for her once
offstage there is no

foreclosure for this no
tender cloud
shovelling.

BIOCHEMICAL ROMANCE

You'd prefer to drift
in a clear prosthetic
tube, rub one of his

umlauts below
the knee, there it is
neither east nor west,

but pidgin flushed
at the tip of two
tranquilized icicles,

his second novel
folding method
a plural fugue

surgery of Cygnus
temperature
dysregulation.

Alps bronze on
our saline, we rake
ambivalent fields,

funnels aristocratic
on nightstands
like unassuming bells

no one could ring
a shawl's common ancestor
breaded like a backlog

of taxonomy and promise.
Your locus nothing
like a late leak.

PSEUDO-PLASTIC FLUID

As desired grease herds
withdrawals of troubled
blankets by hiss, bassinets
      a faint
promise of chlorine, quotations
you'd like to sanitize with soft
        tissue, lists of airspace
            our final handful
            for tallow to tacit
chest hairs doll-like inside
the dilation, witness ingress
old heatstroke of its chorine

naturalized, blushing in unit.
      Can you blush
without a host of recessive oxygen
debt? Bones unpairing the seizure
of spray foam? Quota sums cloaca
neighbours fuck

        walls as much as they fuck
        each other on the other
        side of walls, bodyguards
        weatherstripped fever

stationed in ciphered anoraks.
Why did I even shear sight
lines of viscosity,   wistful sinking?
      Lipborn,
we caption carapace, another

singularity colourfast
in the SeaWorld version,
rolled baroque as blueprints
of alternate underarms, your candling

    limit catalogues secondary
    line to seafloor and base
    coats hour the amniotic
    crucial fix of postponed

    mohair before motels
    at one in the morning
    but barely a hundred
    and one. We charge

palatine to make heel
chalk like eel, a first
counterpoint of silicone
coolant a squeal

of a squash
court, vein-play of Italy
spooning the Tyrrhenian
Sea, venous from miles

oh scab of flight
simulator withholds scansion
handshakes under an engine
of rose bushes, suède-built,

a stingray tweeze
of anatomy around
the temples
do you ever think

about that part
of me my badmouth
abyssal my grayscale
aerial as cloth.

REQUISITION VILLAIN

A ransom of crease   as if trained
in a shuffle of refrigerators, outlines
a bevel of cauliflower and regression
of full wet clouds, ultrasound gel
on your underwear caterwaul dim
       typical of the air-conditioned
click of his mouth,   west where burst

      stuffing is unoccupied, artificial
as pillows that cancel / haunches / look, this MRI
       is a magnetised casket, open
ended passerine of heel release

            above ground
      pool
surface to schedule. Isn't it
    mutually overslept
lockets?   Isn't it the heart
of satellites   emptied
of all metals? Secondhand stark of plaque
   can't be natural
      radioactive
  decay   letterheads in advance

      where updrafts ionised

   their finality / depolarised headwater
   when you first hear
   corneas' sand mimicry   brutalise itself
in corners /   assumed estate.

SOMATOSENSORY EVOKED

Horns admit
centrelines, cyborg
corsage. Adrenal
sets gloved in the single

matter of Potemkin
coming to coils in animal
models of conduction, his eyepatch
the radish-soft lateral

of my departures, ulnar will.
Disconjugate condensation
the modern pout in a type
of radio balance. Electrodes clog

blood, leukocytes loose drum skins
flapping muted and mutated
without swabs of Siberian consent,
cingulate up the anodal

they flash through postures
of thick hair, permanent
pacing the patience of pink
blankets, three millivolts.

Astrocytes in a vase
that suggest this
is a soundless branch
of duplicate marionettes

where daisies could be
as if you bumped
against space, a common
deletion.

AFTERCARE

Are we estranged, immortal
jellyfish medulla on the finger

pads slurred cold crescents
faddish under early crusts

of its dressing the first year
I found gauze where eau de

toilette is final, faints
with annuity of manes,

the blank of cauterized strokes
banal with preservation a damp

lingot of pity and middle
distance hung as if off cortex,

eyes don't have bags
they have life rafts,

inflatable, fleshy brittle
stars how they script

and shingle, conjoined twin
standards our Liszt a little

linden epoxy leans scavenged.
Umbilical did etude diurnal

scale. Motif lemon balm, Melissa
officinalis passenger

her place in eaves, sinus
of canal warble old snow

victimized wreath in wreath
out open-mouthed sea pen

grand guignol find you, an imprint
of plasticity survives me, plural.

AS ASPIRATED

Home base is a block of imitation
ice, in tone or liability above the lip
lukewarm leavens the welter and door
prize longhand since the last election —
mutatis mutandis, the first neurologist

remains an alibi of glial exposures,
the second raw bracket thirsts glass
to airtight genus gathered ovate
indent for her: two wetlands fade
to rostral captions of your brain.

BONE DENSITY

Thread count a ration across her initial
devotion to mammals, the suspended
string of a kite. Posture passed over
at the rate of thin air. Shorebirds —

hour hand their driftwood
through the process of elimination
in my clock shirt — the shirt
with the frozen time

pieces aired over
heated sand; the plasma
of an anesthesiologist's
posthumous tomato script

manifesting a state of captivity
the length of the sleeve a funnel
cloud of surgical inclines — never
hit as they thought it would.

FRENCH REVOLUTION

I watched the live action
version of *Alice in Wonderland*.
It came with the cereal. I grew
confused and inherited
the apartment with fistfuls

of red table grapes from each
synthetic nurse, a flyover
until I can wet the sum
like a quote. My citron a seal
of interim perspective — grain
height hysteria in tenth-grade

art you somehow grind into
a chagrin of milk illocution
until you can forecast lactic
tempers. Queue blue jays
in a sauceboat, and it's still
a counterpoise.

MUSIC FOR TWO OR MORE TURTLES

Strike your magus, I'm an ant
from the colony my marrow
his captive towels tucked in

come waterhole, mouthfuls
pick single lenses come feed
me into simple iodine

arrangements, stiff sensory
migrations, come ocellis,
nook my regulatory

hamster bond its compound
eye, cortices pair trophy
with base ladles —

I'm one of those, sergeant,
the schoolgirl, the fast
food killer, conditions

we bend our uptake
flak to basics
purely instrumental

organelles clenched
to clefs under which
windpipe pink phases

microbleeds for these
crepuscular rays I was
upsell in my molar, Gulliver,

pacinian tenants since
arson discerns, he drove
hollow duo hunter's steel

and trap strays
direct titanium—
shallow and even.

FORM INTAKE

Though the word is count there are no numbers
that start with C. The French use *cent* so can count
marks on a scale like loose change, a circulation
of census. Centuries obey the docudrama, the head
      is not submerged. The zero aligns
          closer to her
      handwriting   if she drops
her arm like a checkmark
      on a chart, the limit
         of a winter's
wide spine. So little of anyone eating their own
      appetite of knees. Last minutes
          are off-white, fingers bowed balance
              of centaur   surcharge
    a substituted invasion.

LYSIS AND REGISTRATION

i. *Hydrolysis*

Neural dial inlets of mascara
fleck frazil when hassled, grease
ice on the legibility of life, laces,
loss of the wonky subtropical hold

audio castles a city vague, branches
base, acid casts knack, my darling
my downpour the reticulated mid
airs kneel cucumber bonds.

Salt remembers, orgasms
mallet of amber, ampere
loose ampersand sheds
gilded freeze calypso

regimes engendered last
stragglers the silverwork
of sciatica thirst to will
a gill's stillness blind.

ii. *Paralysis*

My false skull spools cell
snow, spoils slicks seen
pale from storms, ill sail

strabismus, strategy
counts socket nerves,
squares tin strata

stings wrist spheres
stoics soon swallow
oiled star alalia.

iii. *Analysis*

Briar pairs believe in injectable forms,
her valve's foreign displays of somatic

soil, ester hushed of your novice rind
and stock bisections of delay, the sea

purse manifests its dose early an accent
chair of the city near declared ventricles,

scans weighed my abduction assay, solids
believe in the bias of driftwood.

iv. *Catalysis*

My throat leads me on, narrow home
movie a bag of soil that rears itself

against this poolside
attitude, heredity

answered as airlocks
are prizewinning

cashmere inattention
a breach

in the furnace
and not the resolve

of short saliva,
its rearview manicure.

Quip. That twitch.
What wind of quip.

SAVE THE DATE

Saltwater slides over freshwater,
mimics the look of air and more
becomes involuntary. Hairdresser,
fixated like polynya that won't

melt into itself, straightens her own
hair between customers. Foreheads
blanching her mirror bent bank
signatures — clothed in a balance

sheet, how stunted and arctic
our bodies under the clear line
of a water table, its own substance
drowning beneath, a dead block

from salinity. That's nothing.
Like a babysitter, I take the stairs
one at a time, lift a flashlight
of dying batteries.

ALTERNATE REBELLION

Sterile hounds rush suds to speech
distortion, that northern axon look
a grape of candid calcined limits.
Respiration of rival capitals
snail blanked and treatment naive.
Vague highland of dry drowning

appendage, another first octopus
of conduction tastes with its skin,
the oversleep to these meals. He
believes her equestrian as if ordained
by Kubrick subsequent to himself,
hair fetal as exhaust pipes

a honeymoon slur
of jello slur *au
revoir* silky a salt
marsh, its scale-
like leaves. Grey gosh a second use
for a livery. Cursive calve glare

sponsors microclimate
of pylon deposits? Is she dying?
Does she wish she could
draw with not much more
than a soda
poured over herself?

HYDRAULIC GRETEL NOCTURNE

Silver thaw resigns endemic, holds a finger
bleed halo of lowboys, the load-bearing town
solo of lint spinal in rebuttal and furious first

floor smoke point. Hairless to scale, commuter
Hansel a crisis of ornament, celsius defaults. All
his sleeper berths resinous with liquidation

of soaps shaped like woodcutter rosebuds
in installments varicose with gasoline
synopsis, lit violet on impasse. One pollen

of liability shines scleral, corners of eyes
conclusive as laundry shoots, insist the white
lines, wanting atoms, break apart, highways

of compound fractures long after
breadcrumbs backtrack, skeletal
with bedrock hurry,

backbone of mechanical folding
goosenecks skin the sequential
backhand of future landing.

HALTINGLY

The beavers at the airport
toyshop pat mechanical
tails like a grounded holiday.

Time limits submit from glance
to glance. I run low on security,
raccoons withdrawn from the trash.

The numbness on the tip
of the tongue doesn't spread,
each swallow in line with itself.

Boarded we sleep like there's nothing
more than a centimetre of space
above us; its thoughts are ours.

CONVEYOR

This is how a lawn runs
from you — it enters
every room at once.

I want to call it
a marionette but it's cut
short and lubricated

with firm light that strikes
your teeth like a tipped glass.
Lost Muppet, I pull

every string, explain it away
— a swimming pool that packs
itself with bodies and asks

if it's raining — it is, the downpour
can't come to any other
conclusion. Oh, is that

what it is, does it come
with a name
it can keep

on a conveyor belt,
suffer it neither
here nor there.

APSIS

Didn't your mother teach you not to practise
so close to home? Find body parts you can
wash with your clothes still on. Leaves you
with hands — no one has strings that long,
eustyle out to sea, or through a broken net.

First off, he was a fisherman, disconnected
like cotton on either end of a swab. He sat
beside the window; we could have run out
of gas. It's the first celestial binary they have
mandatory masks for, sometimes gloves —

surfaces you can't touch when thread juts
through like salmon. But chimneys can add
to the white of an open or starched mouth.
This isn't the last time you can have one
without the other flight home.

PLANET OF THINGS

> *It really is a violent, horribly violent world that is obscure to us because we're encased in neoprene, you know, and we're much larger than that world.*
>
> — WERNER HERZOG, *Encounters at the End of the World*

Hand-to-mouth is the final conscious, required action. Trays set like teeth, our last step forward. We take turns flinging things into the fire. When some objects burn, the flames stream like a detour, turn blue and rush sideways. This happens with soft things that submerge the same under a mouthful of waterway or carp caught with bare hands, fins full of surfacing and flu needles. Soft things made of one spouse. Pinched nerves, bunched newspaper, and unlit storefronts are some examples. Maybe the lumps under the paint itself. Heat on our faces, flames are secondary; the balls of our feet are river stones, as if the next applicant in line would bound with locked knees, as if there were an opposite shore, a smoulder.

WHAT HAPPENED IN VENICE

How an injured window isn't always an icicle
above your head and other toppled placebo.
How the stillicide its border grip and bylaws.
How people with microwaves are gatekeepers
of decency. How they adopt cats from bodegas
name them Agent Orange. How they'll put slices
of me over their sagging eyes. How other hours
blur vision after the last bite. How you should
learn to paint Christmas. How then you could
paint Christmas on revolving doors all diners
resting heads feeble as oyster beds on defeated
arms with hairs setting like the copper sunset
of pipes ripped from walls of a vacant house
how this would be done with a price point how
eating sauerkraut with chopsticks isn't the moon
for me. How you can't deal with the vibrating
toothbrush. How it could be more of a dildo
in your mouth if there was an unboxed dildo,
stunted margins. How I don't know what I think
of giant hamburgers anymore. How distance is
Venice how it's thicker than an eraser. How what
happened in Venice died in Venice. How it's hot
enough that all words sweat through their second
meaning, sequential implications watered-down
elements puddled at our feet how it's an afternoon
appetite you're after.

THE REDSHIFT

Things happen
every day. Cats die.
Men act like your neurons
are pancakes. Some cats
die in your arms
before you have a chance
to put them down. Really,
you're a jump rope,
touching down
half the time. It's easier
to calculate the odds,
the long-run accustomed
to wearing a wetsuit.
Halfway to Alaska
before anyone notices
we're draped
in each other's scarves.
The bananas are larger
here, the books are used
as bedsheets, holes
for our eyes. You can't be more
jealous than the shore
until you stop
holding your breath.
The sun dips
like a tusk, every Cubist
in the glass. Turnstiles
leave nothing
to the imagination —
the most contagious
verbatim vessels,
the limits of a valise.

Whole rooms bristle
like barbecue sauce.
When they're this
impressed, their lips
disappear.

AFOOT

All combat like this
woman, her feet two
bare fighter planes
slipped from loafer
to loafer, clear
wind tunnels. Even
the air-to-air glides
with the chill
of bedridden stunts,
faux fur loses
focus, long naps
a suspension of plastic
artifacts, rival corals.

[LOVEBIRDS I & II]

    for riptides, prescriptions
    in the porcelain water
    fountain, analogous luck
    of colour wheel foreclosure
    fogging the redeye
    a mouthpiece of tourist caves
    a membrane's hemispheric wilt
    a continental nudge of baby carrots
    floors that weren't caudal
    the first airdrop taken for a wedding
    at glandular intervals.

LITHOPEDION LOVE SONG

"An example of monsters that are formed, the mother having remained seated too long, having had her legs crossed, or having bound her belly too tight while she was pregnant."
　　　　— Dr. Ambroise Paré, *On Monsters and Marvels*

Stone baby, no one sold me
on why you didn't fit lineal
dress of shy aisle lookalikes
for grey matter in lieu, your

gradual blackboards
of skin as if you'd lost
both sleeves in a glass
box, plausible leche-

drenched hairnet, blinks
lactic come forty, air foetal
flipped amid ostium of emory.
Superfetate your follicle

auction, calcified charwoman
crest. Cartilage could lease
slipped billiard respiration
of walnuts to its own

brut blood, Roman trimesters.
Didn't they think to file you
down, a more consensual
silt, aragonite embryonic,

pass off your palms
as the switchboard ends of me
turn atomic limestone face
a mural that abandons

peeling tempos of funereal lip,
telecast frowns the last lines
curved to the edges of bowls,
split fluorescence, broadcast mother

boards of the valley, alluvial jars
of pearls crossed capsular, femur
to dense impulse snail. You
lithographer of milked

deadweights, airwaves a pushpin
lech, immiscible with what seems
like scales, statehood, hairline
a cross of spears, spit-sire

marble unruffled by revs
of our tires, a moon's second
detention, overdone ditch.
Perlite bevelled to seed, lit nasal

occlusive, you're a wingding
fontanelle held as a prisoner
would embed keystones
of sodium sheds, their Aprils

concise with rip kernel
your litmus, foreground
soaped luteal a tensile sell
on film pin-boned, set in quotes.

EVERYONE LOVES A SLINKY

It is almost impossible to pry yourself
from the hypnotizing jaws of Slinky.
Almost impossible not to fall
down the stairs after it.

While the other kids were eating glue,
I was getting my tongue
caught in the Slinky.

Half moon pushed
against half moon.
Joined just past their thinnest points,
two crescents conclude —
circular, empty inside. Piles of the same
joined and joined again below.

Stacked stove coils,
hot to the touch,
Slinky can't help
its conduction —
wedlocked, ring by ring.

Cut Slinky in half, each end
writhes and contracts.

Slung it sways elongated, sunk
like a hammock, a cradle, a cold
distended sloth, you
its clinging infant, eyes half-closed
as it swings, blurring
into something gentle and solid.

The only direction it can follow you
is down. Stacked
on one end, it's stable
as a sandbag.

End-over-end, each side unable to catch
and swallow the other, Slinky staggers, a spine
without a spine, looking for its other
half with every step.

Held from one coda, it's a glum trunk,
dragged down by the dough
of its tender corkscrews. It won't leap
like its hard, tense sister, the spring.
The best it can do is droop, fall
all over itself, loose with measured steps —
alive until it stops.

Your eyes try to follow
as Slinky shoots out
to meet him. Your body
drops into its hoops.

It's not warmer inside the Slinky.
Not a womb, it's easier to escape:
pull it apart, stretch it till it lines up
with the horizon.

Tangled, Slinky is kinked like a code,
words trapped in the throat.
Each mouth gaping closer
to the other than ever before.

There's a strand of Slinky inside
me, a helix tumbling down
the steps of my organs.
Starts with the heart, then flattens
its final rings closed at your feet.

You wrap it around
yourself, like anything else
that could stretch that far —
tinsel, a strap-on bomb.

You take a step and Slinky vibrates,
twitches down
your frame, the tangled
crease on your palm, uncovers you
from a winding song.

SIGNS OVER SYMPTOMS

The shell doesn't wait for me
to hang up. It puts housesitters on
hold. We can both be
separate, wired like braces

around the flaws
in my mouth. Ghost grills.
It talks back to the glistening
presence of a Diet Coke

that entered the room
before a neurologist's full
body. I tell it it's made
of something jejune, like head lice,

or popsicle sticks, or vodka
shots on a Lilliputian table
made of popsicle sticks.
It still keeps slurring.

ORGAN DONOR

Call it proof of decimals
shot straight home
in napkins. Snowflakes
slip under the canal
bridge, the water damage
gene that can't be bred
out like the sea level
of a stark, Italian movie.

Call it altitude's last loss. Call
on every iceberg ever bolted
to the brink of a blind black
dress. It doesn't leave
blinks or translations
on our excess. Robotics sees
itself off the lawn —
the buildup

a study in blue, the death
of the number two. Call off
blindfolds that demonstrate
how to shrink a heavy hex
nut or expand a wing nut;
how to shuffle like a suitcase.
So what if hints of ventilation
end up all over our menus?

We would have kept an arc
of paper dolls in the freezer.
The white collapse disturbing
the drift with nothing
to declare but the full spread

of your ventriloquist's arms.
Introduce a chair and people
act as normal as possible.

Wrapping paper offers parental
advice, falls asleep with a voice
in the room; a certain age
locks its spine to the twist
of a cruller, the chug
and chirping stone's throw
of that public station. Shine,
scrap heap, shine.

ASTROBLEME ANODYNE

All homecomings
    survive outside the body
the wounds of binoculars
    celebrate with glamour
of retired bird breeders
    a bulge of breeze dental
in the itch of quotation marks
    straw sweat our sincere capillary
at the border we're asked to sketch
    civil formation its dull lavender
weight churchy through ice
        a regression lozenge
    to another self her rocket
        popsicle gradual
    from duplicate
        distance.

TENDERIZER

Hair at sea urchin,
its most repetitive
barrels borne down

on hardened cranial
nerves rival flicks
of uncapped pens

bisect their faces, a compass
of compromised zoology:
the fine young caramels,

boxes of hawthorn blood
pinch you apart how
a breezeway is first to be

particle through bluer
flasks never the formulae
of any common resident's

shrunken subsea but our own
false memories coral-grown
vulnerable lacuna waste

sockets of solid sand dollars
previous new money
floodlights my castor

balletics, sieved pedicellariae
as instructed we'd love
to be winterized

with vasculature on the front
steps, or a lid pulled vagrant,
televised from long leather,

lipstick funded with shades
of loading docks. Better to exist
in agarose well plates than living

ankles sensitized with clay
degeneration, your reflex
hammers dead ringers for split

screens with meat
tenderizers fathers
weld for wives

before I can see
into sinks, the cold
left running

for cutaneous
and superficial
response.

UNDER THE TABLE

She should have undressed in public;
they've added sporadic gargoyles
into the décor. Here and there a face
takes her in; its eyes the same stone
colour as its body, unflinching, overall
grey the far-off sound of a dog's bark.
A bark that comes on mileage,
thumps of disposed munitions, curbs
of dragged loads. It's a dog's first work,
not being seen from the street like a week
that follows with nothing, then remains
landscaping, or at least a clue
for it, a clipped series of blades that stop
the barking. It's not warmer
inside; they've left the heat off, her father
makes ice in Kingston for two
dollars an hour under the table.
Early, insulted, gloved,
walls freeze with the passing
of each shift, gelid bags sealed
with the density of dropped voices
he left behind to be here, the State's
weekly quota of offal, a roll
of tobacco the length of a man
broken down into cigarettes, stacked
amongst itself and kids that soften
kidneys and sighs past queues that yield
loud as the stiffness of the well
rehearsed tar on the balcony.
They have years of practise
between each sentence and play

detached taillights
on their way home.

OLD TIMES

Lack leaves enough. She tells them she came with the strand
beside the empty chair. They nod, as if she'd used her head
for indication. If you snap she could take things in fast enough;
the lake could always look as allelic, always fill itself with delays,
something as basic

> as swimming to shore with bones for lashes, or not
> being able to strain her neck enough for this. If you
> snap the wrong thing on the subway platform, not
> having much of a memory for cactuses, yellow
>
> trumpets, sometimes, Baileys and bugles
> exhaust me. Succulents exhaust me, a song
> about wigs stuck indoors for days. So what
> if we're grazed as gist? Membranes the ellipsis
> of repertoire exhaust me.

Your coatroom looks like pencil crayons, and headlocks. We sleep on
the air mattress — days of this, then more. It has a motor, a set
of Pinter legs that self-inflate like my own. You say you feel industry
through primal sleeves, folded in flocks of you. Nothing changes.

ALLOSTATIC LOAD

Something fell on her
(it was just the natural
sweetness of a receipt),
her first finger bowl
could have filtered

steps around morning
construction crews,
semi-sheer, under eye
honour. Still the serum
alarm never littoral

with monitored starfish
sects, but that made it
up of overgrown wash,
a wet she walked
alongside the flight

decks. What are you like
her therapist? Fresh hoodie
for spring? Barely there bed
papaya can't distinguish
from an abundance

of chernozem or the kind
of sex that sounds minted
like the morning after
a Seinfeld routine, definitive
semaphore downturn.

Have you towelled the aluminum
revenge of anything? This brief stem
accelerated its own starry kitten
heel, glue subtle, esophageal
publicly related though not

to hints that turn
with their deadlock and diets
of hyper batter, bolt counts, and toddler
puffs. Laxative fondlers

their last thumbnail
suggestive of slurred clovers
where drains should be
foxholes, buffed nails
a backslash of envelopes

at the cellular level
all I want is to listen
to you play basketball,
eat around the bad
parts of apples, an echo

of fibres the tall ask after
your hair evens out. I should
live among their socks so as not
to arouse suspicion, the unposed
never as old as legibility

and airmen of extended water
fasts, burn marks repurposed
as theft, geranium spillway
the speedometers of surface
vessels, your draughty camera.

THEIR NURSE NAUTICAL

This won't help
her, her house
has first aid
kits, their clasps
locked thaw

      like waiting
whitefly waist,
      injury in flume

acerose on our
      ruby roux our curbs
shell lethal as hearing

      aids that don't
burn symbiotic
      ducts she sheaths

clocks with a slip-
mouth cold glow
from its throat
for our sweat
to pearl dorsal.

AVAILABLE EMOTICONS

Some all-Americans are fifteen
            minutes and pass
for the Geraldo sessions
            drinking phones
like soggy ankles in the dark.

Some founders are carousels
            of mitochondria,
a bird's closed coordinates
toughened with coughs.
            Why stop the raw

sponge of noiseless
myelination — for one
            morning a crush
of thumbprint, bleached
            heatstroke.

DRESSED FABULOUSLY IN WEEDS

The ice cream man's
      militaristic twinkle
twinkle little contusion
      the stars in his submenu
start bright   absolved from the neck
this way   if you have a strait
you have an ovary worry
      one sensually
           radioactive plant panel,
           lullabies within
southwest injury of conversational sun
      the pupas bleach forks
their composite
      in distant futures I started with
      snow cones severe hairdos
around stirrups   nettle accents
an ignition
      of fan fiction   retouched peels

THE SIZE OF WATCH MOVEMENTS

Minute hands their own
fossil boundary.

Is every other line a lumberyard
returned to itself? Look, I can't be

watered, moon-phase rotating
apertures, send mild

traumatic Sour Keys and special
certificates. The art or science

of measuring time is just shy
of vestigial, the bubblegum

aorta under coveted slots
at virology summits

matured to blood
thinners, a blister

of underserved sundials.
Calibre squint subordinate

ligne, Swiss or pacified metric
would an ichnite in spring.

HE DIDN'T KNOW WHERE ANYTHING WAS

After leaving him I walked two blocks
behind three girls. The one in the middle
lagged a step or more and made phone call

after phone call. She said her sweat stains
were heart-shaped and the phone lifted
along with her arms. Heels quick like dips

in a finger bowl, she caught up, collapsed
the triangle and screamed, Love you! I love
you! with a strict, drunk plank on either side.

As a line they dragged nothing, a storefront
on the right. Its sign stripped to the charge
of residual glue, floor a suffocation

of black garbage bags huddled in rumour.
They blinked in and out of heat like a herd
of charcoal encouraged with a series of blows.

OUTLIVING LANTERNS

This late in the season, everything
debunks chemical, comb
snug at the bottom of her purse.

It's secure for plastic — bits of hair knotted
with resistance of folded towels. The kind
she'd pull out when a hairline or sequel

would be enough to adjust dents
in the dark cold. As if the finishing touches
were inhospitable or just kissing, snowed in

closer to machines — hips as laboratory,
clumps of midriffs the browned bones
of our tires, their posture tube, their splash.

Snow balds like a leap, pigeoned,
untouchable as suspenders. Her house
no longer needs a key. Tiptoes set the code

for a security lock. Each beep bridges
a settlement. Sounds like she's trying
to microwave contents of the house but can't

draw water, conclusions, remember the power
level; her finger divides one volume between
them, warm, braise, reheat, defrost.

WOULDN'T DREAM OF IT

He can't keep track of this eclipse any more
than the high beams of idle cars excusing
its grandstand of calendar, table salt shorthand

of iron-stunned snow underfoot not his
dreamer patted dry; our legs
dangle as tablecloths, resolve of fishing

rods neural over appetite, slugs a fear
surrogate for nurtured wigs. Dendrite
is primitive — pale decibel windscreen

stands by for stand-ins nothing like rain;
they care where they fall they could boil
in the thick of a plug a mutual paraphrase.

THE ORIGIN OF PRACTICALITY

1.

It's not possible to put a phone down;
we dream of a waste dump, in waking
it isn't meant to carry more sound, fly
out when we turn magnolias to leave,
and our tenses shrivel, how cranial
nerves can be third, flames flattened
against the Erie canal like an animal
hides the pink of its ears, Virginia

> Woolf upright as a letterbox, she
> saved herself from a war, locked
> stones felled heads in pockets.
> An excellent swimmer, she was

fifty-nine; these anvils are children,
saturated under awnings of milk
bars, each not knowing floorboards,
Noah's Ark, what the other bought
(bruised fruit, cotton balls), talk
of tax sleep in their form, peopled
a pace seahorse, tail a discount
curl around seabottom weeds.

2.

It's a shrivel dreaming of a nerve's waste,
and our tenses condition. They say war,
locked stones into awnings, floorboards,
Noah's Ark. The other at a cranial pace,
and we turn her around from an excellent

swimmer. She was Erie form; ear people
are cotton balls, ready with seahorse. Her
pockets not meant to look down sound,
Noah's bruised tax and they felled, under
the process of discount fruit, waves curled

magnolia. We're inclined, quiet only later,
in condition Virginia Woolf; she saved
some sleep in tenses, children, each not
knowing a landfill loudly, then the hand
a city's floorboard, our tenses bought.

3.

It isn't meant to carry any more sound.
The landfill goes, only later, dreaming,
piled the way we came, saying Virginia
Woolf was brave, she saved her pockets.
She was a excellent anvil, which talked
of quiet in its sleep, saying, once you
undertow at a walking nerve, tallow
the waves, tail curled around the space
of heads when possible put a telephone
down an ark, inclined like locked stones,
where wrinkle out of it, we turn letterbox
her tenses, and our pockets canal. She
was fifty-nine; these people are leaving
a milk bar, filled like tax forms, seabottom
weeds shrivel out from sound, felled
back to anvils.

4.

It's a waking stone, this milk around an excellent swimmer.
A landfill damp bodies in an ark, the space of sleep, tallow

bruised with the waves of pockets, when we turn, Virginia
Woolf was saturated to pick things up, our rest cure, animal

fat. Pace your seabottom weeds. Condition ark, a tail curled
without water, cotton balls wrinkle telephone possible. War

milk waves sleep from our tenses, an anvil's pink children
bought landfills of Noah's hand floating like quiet thoughts

of the awning. Your discount bruise of flames looking down
loudly: a city, a war, conversation forms pressed to filled soil.

5.

Herself a war, when possible
discount curled under children

to landfill upright like animal fat,
telephone condition felled

    pink from sun; pockets
    locked ear canals.

6.

Waking of cotton, ark children, she saved herself
from a saturated swimmer, meant bruised nerve
soil, herself a tallow leave. Heads milk tenses
of seahorse discount, excellent turn.

BLOODSHOTS

The root vegetable takes its own shelf
life. What does that make me? Painted
grey and dressed like lichen to sleep in.

Park patrol dimmed grids
of misunderstanding. Starch circuit.
Hoof of the soundless sun. Potatoes

are eighty percent water, champagne,
or Tetris; have two chromosomes
more than humans. Headlamps peer

into dry, dark storage. Depots lonely
on their way up past our necklines.
Once released, ponytails are sleeping

habits, contagious as zippers
you need help with drawing
to the back of your neck, moon

more situated than an absence
of seals, the time they don't take.
I don't belong in a turnpike. I'm turning

all these eggs again. I mean, I'm eating
all these whites — they're anonymous
as seatbelts, archives of ice. The ignition

turns them cardinal; they lose
identification, some other things
you knew about me already.

ROMAN HOLIDAY

She bit the inside of her mouth
into flaps. She wants people to test
the wholeness of their hands
in a wall with a jaw that could snap

a wrist clean of itself, the barber
cutting in. Is it really so wrong
to watch the busboys spill what's left
down the front of their pants?

Is it really so wrong
that their real joke isn't swiping
drinks as soon as anyone looks
away, but how much they like to rub

her back, hands hard as mints
popped from an even harder tin, as she
asks where they stashed her last glass,
the one she didn't stand

a chance with.
She makes the busboys say things
back to her, *Don't watch me go beyond
that corner*, and they repeat just the way

she wanted, adding, *Promise me*.
Was it really so wrong to plan an evening
around Edith Head? What about how
she wanted the inside of her mouth

to look when done — hidden, half-full, sticky
with prints only few busboys will ever see
again, clean of itself.

DO YOU WANT MY POSTAL CODE?

Tide over the final bloom
of pet rocks, departure
lounges, mouth to narrator.

I'll wear socks until it's impossible
to be fluent. Cold hands on clearance.
In the other pocket: Scotch

mints have their reasons, not a stretch
of highway goes bald. All I have
are window displays and negativity

is not something that depends
on room for cream, locations
finalized as biceps. May as well start

fixating on street lamps to even out.
With what flourish I'll mark my card.
Here's to letting my lime loose

while pumping gas! Hiccup
quality an upholstery heist
for the household.

KEPT TIME

A coin with a profile is one abbreviation
for how my lips don't move. The empty

commands of aftertaste — headlights
chaperone bare explanations tightened

to winter curbs. No directories, a recess
of busy signals has the same shoulders.

THIS POSSESSION

I'm a suitable birth
certificate that isn't
suspended like a lullaby

from a statue that has me
mistaking lightning for dehydration
that adopted daylight time

as one would a roadside Russian
blue that takes to unmade beds,
the limits of Goya's subdued

palette. A new birth
heeding me with a discreet
ribcage that says goodbye

in public line-ups. Surnames
pleochroic endings onto civil
lolite, a pasted phrase, another

moonstone, lustre livestock,
sear reversed and carrying
sunlight through its animal.

THE EMPEROR

You not being Arrau crowds
my rushed hands. Pupils
aim perfume at their pulse
points, the straight posture
of a knuckle of light, hung
stomach, or visible water
tanks in the washroom.

Throughout the day
heart notes oversleep
on wrists stiff with hawks,
each dream of takeoff; lift citrus,
unobtrusive as a closed cupboard
by the bedside, not so much
as a protruding soundboard.

FARADAY DARK SPACE

Every other slap
and sleeve stuck
against a one-off
plump as an ice
cube always wet
at the cuff the main
voltage a loose
artery nails turn
pink without sun
trace profit two
fingers congested
as hammers Faraday!
Faraday! on the long
sides of the bridge
slats a postmark killer
cancel till potable
seawater plain
as farm dogs
on the floor —
so full of hands
neither leg
of the startled
namesake a cold
cathode of its
own. Find shade.

APOLLINARIAN AFTER

Outline the temporary
side effects at the clinic,
an optional plugged yard
hose bulging below
the lowest part
of a makeshift shelter,
elbowroom pushing
through a night aligned

as a silhouette of stamps
face-value up, eyes
a perforated, adhesive weight.
In a public washroom, unfold
warnings in the accordion
squares of a pamphlet
sealing two pills — cyclical
disturbances, mastalgia may

occur. May not, Doctor.
They don't come — nothing
comes to the numb
impression of wet, curling
husbandry and its animal
as fast as it's named. It says heresy.
Heresy, from the Greek
to choose. You can't

legislate a material
world. Turn down
the volume. Keepers
beat snow from eaves
and it sounds

like a muffled species
of gunshots, near misses
on the melting ground.

PASSIVE TRANSGRESSIVE

Like a patronymic, water strands
the cuticle, until it's just a spool

of pavement starry with that cobalt,
a feast to discontinue like the blue

hour, how you care about your suit
fit after the crash. This last accident

has no way to make ice cubes,
or fugue states. My gamey energy

company never sends emery boards,
only past due notices, the subsidiary

shell for the colloquialism
of lozenges our jewel-deep tributary

of nail beds. I'm macerating
a migraine of blackberries

to Method Man, after a few
forks the pills start to stick

to the sides of the bottle,
rehearsal reptile

reserves, clips soften
the same distance, stiff clap

dramatized the decorative.
Senseless emulsions have done

better this year, occasional
metal clinked against its copy —

leant arc of lambent
bystanders, Paradol in grown

genders swapped for casualty
of eyelid hides, view buttery

adrenals after the pulse
of driftwood whiskered,

sultry in an overvalue
of winter star charts, before each

script had wide wrists, the chaptered
exuberance of curtains. This salicylate

wants to site me but you can
eat a lot of stone fruit

in an afternoon, immaculately attach
electrodes to every non-emergency

number, hairlike with the minute
moon of your purse, which is just

one coupled follicle before it
so much as rains.

ATOMZAHL

We are a reveal of grass swollen
with veins and the supervised
play of final servings, eels pupil-
black with curve of bureaucrat

filtration is statues in autumn
substitution over simple lungs
our volley damp with transplant,
a pastel sterilized with straps

of aunts, jackal ash, muzzles
retain water as rivulet weight
wrenches damsel endothelial
from between our legs backdrops

slipped like onion skins, white images
of mucin in longcase mocking
from the waist men wear
their atomic number.

ATHEIST STAPLERS

Soft carrots are breath hunger in afterlife
of sun resettling porcelain on a deflation
come honest moths historical from saliva

eclipse surface tension tamed lustring
camouflage in the lungs a ratio
of undersides and benches pliable as algid

staggers of stitches the state says naked
as a silkworm a summer incision glass
carte blanche leaves pause her airways

matinees and axes of pacific
spheres by staple vernacular
by brow by patent met supple

in sericulture thread is ignition
and pulmonary hair grows apart
from horsemen static that reins

transparency of moisture I neglect
how fleshless a dose to the chintzy
albumin carried queue

of celluloid murmur to his collar
a seal of paraffin around the lip
of the test tube that holds

Edison's last breath undying
miniature of suffocation
reduced from a synthesis of bedsides.

CLOUDS LIKE ICE

If the wires drift like surface ice inside you,
        there's no other brindle
in the sea lapse with an incisor / guise
            to its colour agent. There is no stent
        outbreak for a decimal
of folding chairs. The flesh fraction
      of midmorning
ice cubes in our glass an addressable grey
      of clouds like untied laces
        that defer to St. Hilda's siamese
connection, trail off into an accrual of tubs
      before forming their own
stopover,   the busywork of bloodlines only
a synthetic bloodshot ago   clouds a middle
child wringing her hair distant   brass from air
    corridors this one
             an atmosphere
    of plain embalming fluid   chirps
       in a pigtail of sky   postpones itself
    a puddle of keys. Looks down
aerosol showrooms   femur propellants willow recent
   with each ashen flash
    of swallow. Overcast glass depth / our ice a tier
        clouds shipwrecked
   to scale   unshaven with titular palisades
       outlying mandibles in spacesuit
   union, flock scruff
of beds for the night one
by capsize an isolation   of sound
             is a standard of straw.

AS COLD AS YOU THOUGHT IT WAS

The sand didn't suffice, it had to
be warmed, and formal

like a clean shaven face.
You arched your way

into death, as wet gravel
would arch withstanding

the hypotheses of worn
leather, the pure hide

watering the bareness
of your footsteps before winter

daylight could reach its own
length, your mattress kissing

the wall — one straight line
the aftertaste of another

PARTIAL NUDITY

Ornithology over the flake
of sunburn has less trouble
with people when they say,
I'm learning to fall
asleep on my back or, Death

of Marat — he was writing
a list of names in that bath.
Avocet in the wet
season a stack of personal
cheques, hyphenated eyes

a third estate: a bubble
between two panels
has to make friends
with the pilot,
airborne disguise.

SKIN FOUNDATION CHAIRS

Shirt holes want cubic controls,
their hometowns cool sonar
to the keyless, overruled puree

of wrinkled exam
table paper and no reply
to the cinematic nature

of summer colds. I impress inguinal
echoes onto new olive widths,
wrenched eyelid

instructions — the overheated
withhold on a sense
of lavender, its insect

temperatures open and close
like a stranded cashbox, only
for documentation of eye colour

a sonographer's glacier
shoes for ultrasounds
in tiled basements, sweat

of a bat, bolted
vinyl the lightest shade of skin
foundation, winter cherry

ignition draws slack tongues
left pale no fingerful of night.
It's an ice shelf lie back

on a second
of echolocation, an overhead
of clean hands. The buses glow

cumulus and you
give yourself something
other than light to squint at.

RUSTLE HEMATOLOGY

The blood work lab redirects her
along one of its lengths. Its lobby
the immediacy of a wall-mounted
mattress, a train cabin's denial.

Walking frames enter almanacs,
displacing airdates antiquated
as a sliding door uniformity
that faces hers. Each floor breaks

into a blank of sacrum or peplum
in full assent of what overwhelms
her features. Voices lining
their minerals.

MEAN CORPUSCULAR VOLUME

Rain a substitute
roll call, a display
of lowered arms.
You could be

doubled over
the features of four
birds facing the inside
of a burial jar, skulls

replaced with rings
of cone shells, hand
cupped over carbon
dating, smudge of solved

fractions, multiples
of plasma, most water.
The usual Sunday
tourniquet straps blood

vessels like strands of hair
from a face, radial
arteries roll away
under the bed

of your skin. Nurse
as chatty as a braid
binding itself to itself
on the way down.

HUMOUR MAINTENANCE

Bloodletting is a tall man
measured in hand widths
when ripe plum skin isn't
much more than broken
sleep on a flat of moonlet
somnolence that tastes
like soap or its standby
music, the curvature
of earth initialed
to complete bloodletting
measured when sleep isn't
much more than ripe
plum skin stencilled
to complete nocturne,
non-invasive sheets
of airspeed formalities. Bloodlust
is a swimsuit that appears
tear-shaped in thumbnails,
endangered reef red
swimsuit in a window,
  BAE WATCH
from bust to navel. Not bloodless,
but spooled as if an anastatica
miscalculation of a nebula.
How does a person
  sleep? How
does a person remember
how. There's no aerating
spine in common with erasure
as quick as shattered winter
melon loosening its injury
of wet seeds surge the dehisce

of stars, a hierarchy of rain levers
melted down for backwash
of inside flesh to partial sun
a marlin so modern you're asked
to take root in the counterpoint
twist of elapsed towels, silhouette
a softcore for parachuting in
a combustion of refined sugar
dreaming at the spine and false
rose of Jericho the first apostle
that subtracts cauterized solar
missing the point we dream
of evidence, the watered down
sleep of evidence.

FLUENCY OF OVERBITES

I've developed a taste for bland food.
Under powdery light, cauliflower
is an ancestor, a first-grader
depicting shirtless ennui

of x-rays, wing-stains a license,
CYBEAR, or RHEUMY
Cadillac, lamella head counts
outside disease progression

offshore, outpatient,
portion cups offer pills
or tartar sauce, a breed
of unoccupied linoleum

in the ailing middle of bleach
due to go under. Overbites
a submissive submarine or elastic
like raw dough or an individual

neurology that can't be
coaxed skylights, contracted
orderlies facing front in the way
you know you've known it.

ACKNOWLEDGMENTS

Awed thanks to everyone at Anvil Press for their unwavering vim and belief in my writing. Thanks to thoughtful Cloud for every light-touch glimmer and abiding shaft of light. Thanks to my father for my teeth and metaphors, my mother for their unconditional aeration. Thank you to my grandfather for the watercolour of Poland that kept me company throughout this book's creation. To M.M for Finn, again!, the gifts at the concierge. Thanks to Cassidy for being vivid and earthborn. With untold appreciation to Lorna Crozier and Bill Gaston for keystone seeing and for insights past. (Thanks to Brian Hendricks for the dream of uncertainty.) Thanks to Ben for harks of enthusiasm and for being a colour-coded treasure who's never not been. Thanks to X.A. for sudden theories of herringbone and for discernment and for Pt. Hope infiltration. Thanks to Aerie for the bells and laurels of rabarbar, the tricky U, dancing L, and wonderful W. Thanks to anyone who has ever caught my eyes jump, in examination or Carpathian.

Thank you to The Ontario Arts Council for providing a Writers' Reserve Grant which helped in the writing of this book.

I am grateful to the respective editors of the following publications in whose pages some of these poems appeared, at times in (slightly or radically) different iterations: *The Capilano Review, CV2, The Maple Tree Literary Supplement, This Magazine, Poetry is Dead.*

ABOUT THE AUTHOR

Born in Istanbul, Caroline Szpak is a Polish-Canadian writer who lives in Toronto. A graduate of the University of Victoria writing program, her poetry and fiction have appeared in *This Magazine, The Capilano Review, subTerrain, Poetry is Dead, CV2*, and in the chapbooks *Expense Account, Garland Get Your Gun,* and *The Pomeranian Front. Slinky Naive* is her first collection of poetry.